Collins

by Iain Gray

LangSyne
PUBLISHING
WRITING *to* REMEMBER

E-mail: info@lang-syne.co.uk

Distributed in the Republic of Ireland by Portfolio Group,
Kilbarrack Ind. Est. Kilbarrack, Dublin 5.
T:00353(01) 839 4918 F:00353(01) 839 5826
sales@portfoliogroup.ie
www.portfoliogroup.ie

Design by Dorothy Meikle   Printed by Ricoh Print Scotland

ISBN 978-1-85217-246-6

Collins

MOTTO:
The wounds of life
(and) By valour and skill.

CREST:
A pelican.

NAME variations include:
Ó Coileáin *(Gaelic)*
Ó Cuilleáin *(Gaelic)*
O'Collins
O'Cullane
Cullane
Collinson

Chapter one:

Origins of Irish surnames

According to an old saying, there are two types of Irish – those who actually are Irish and those who wish they were.

This sentiment is only one example of the allure that the high romance and drama of the proud nation's history holds for thousands of people scattered across the world today.

It's a sad fact, however, that the vast majority of Irish surnames are found far beyond Irish shores, rather than on the Emerald Isle itself.

The population stood at around eight million souls in 1841, but today it stands at fewer than six million.

This is mainly a tragic consequence of the potato famine, also known as the Great Hunger, which devastated Ireland between 1845 and 1849.

The Irish peasantry had become almost wholly reliant for basic sustenance on the potato, first introduced from the Americas in the seventeenth century.

When the crop was hit by a blight, at least 800,000 people starved to death while an estimated two million others were forced to seek a new life far from their native shores – particularly in America, Canada, and Australia.

The effects of the potato blight continued until about 1851, by which time a firm pattern of emigration had become established.

Ireland's loss, however, was to the gain of the countries in which the immigrants settled, contributing enormously, as their descendants do today, to the well being of the nations in which their forefathers settled.

But those who were forced through dire circumstance to establish a new life in foreign parts never forgot their roots, or the proud heritage and traditions of the land that gave them birth.

Nor do their descendants.

It is a heritage that is inextricably bound up in the colourful variety of Irish names themselves – and the origin and history of these names forms an integral part of the vibrant drama that is the nation's history, one of both glorious fortune and tragic misfortune.

This history is well documented, and one of the most important and fascinating of the earliest sources are *The Annals of the Four Masters*, compiled between 1632 and 1636 by four friars at the Franciscan Monastery in County Donegal.

Compiled from earlier sources, and purporting to go back to the Biblical Deluge, much of the material takes in the mythological origins and history of Ireland and the Irish.

This includes tales of successive waves of invaders and settlers such as the Fomorians, the Partholonians, the Nemedians, the Fir Bolgs, the Tuatha De Danann, and the Laigain.

Of particular interest are the *Milesian Genealogies*,

The 'golden age' of the Gaelic-Irish clans, infused as their veins were with the blood of Celts, pre-dates the Viking invasions of the eighth and ninth centuries and the Norman invasion of the twelfth century, and the sacred heart of the country was the Hill of Tara, near the River Boyne, in County Meath.

Known in Gaelic as 'Teamhar na Rí', or Hill of Kings, it was the royal seat of the 'Ard Rí Éireann', or High King of Ireland, to whom the petty kings, or chieftains, from the island's provinces were ultimately subordinate.

It was on the Hill of Tara, beside a stone pillar known as the Irish 'Lia Fáil', or Stone of Destiny, that the High Kings were inaugurated and, according to legend, this stone would emit a piercing screech that could be heard all over Ireland when touched by the hand of the rightful king.

The Hill of Tara is today one of the island's main tourist attractions.

Opposition to English rule over Ireland, established in the wake of the Cambro-Norman invasion, broke out frequently and the harsh solution adopted by the powerful forces of the Crown was to forcibly evict the native Irish from their lands.

These lands were then granted to Protestant colonists, or 'planters', from Britain.

Many of these colonists, ironically, came from Scotland and were the descendants of the original 'Scotti', or 'Scots', who gave their name to Scotland after migrating there in the fifth century A.D., from the north of Ireland.

Colonisation entailed harsh penal laws being imposed on the majority of the native Irish population, stripping them practically of all of their rights.

The Crown's main bastion in Ireland was Dublin and its environs, known as the Pale, and it was the dispossessed peasantry who lived outside this Pale, desperately striving to eke out a meagre living.

It was this that gave rise to the modern-day expression of someone or something being 'beyond the pale'.

Attempts were made to stamp out all aspects of the ancient Gaelic-Irish culture, to the extent that even to bear a Gaelic-Irish name was to invite discrimination.

This is why many Gaelic-Irish names were anglicised with, for example, and noted above, Ó Ceallaigh, or O'Kelly, being anglicised to Kelly.

Succeeding centuries have seen strong revivals of Gaelic-Irish consciousness, however, and this has led to many families reverting back to the original form of their name, while the language itself is frequently found on the fluent tongues of an estimated 90,000 to 145,000 of the island's population.

Ireland's turbulent history of religious and political strife is one that lasted well into the twentieth century, a landmark century that saw the partition of the island into the twenty-six counties of the independent Republic of

Ireland, or Eire, and the six counties of Northern Ireland, or Ulster.

Dublin, originally founded by Vikings, is now a vibrant and truly cosmopolitan city while the proud city of Belfast is one of the jewels in the crown of Ulster.

It was Saint Patrick who first brought the light of Christianity to Ireland in the fifth century A.D.

Interpretations of this Christian message have varied over the centuries, often leading to bitter sectarian conflict – but the many intricately sculpted Celtic Crosses found all over the island are symbolic of a unity that crosses the sectarian divide.

It is an image that fuses the 'old gods' of the Celts with Christianity.

All the signs from the early years of this new millennium indicate that sectarian strife may soon become a thing of the past – with the Irish and their many kinsfolk across the world, be they Protestant or Catholic, finding common purpose in the rich tapestry of their shared heritage.

Chapter two:

The young warriors

While Collins is a surname with more than one source of origin and while one of these sources is the English name denoting 'son of Colin', the other sources are rooted deeply in the ancient soil of Ireland.

One Gaelic form of the name is Ó Coileáin, and this sept was originally centred in the area of North Desmond in the province of Munster.

The name stems from the Gaelic 'coilean', said to denote a young whelp or hound, or a young warrior, and this connects to the legendary Irish hero Cúchulainn – also known as The Hound of Ulster or the Hound of Culann.

The semi-legendary hero is believed to have lived in the first century AD, and was first known as Setanta, indicating he may have belonged to a tribe known as the Setantii, while some sources assert he was a direct descendant of the Ó Coileáin.

In his legendary aspect his father is the Celtic sun god Lugh, and Cúchulainn himself became revered as a sun divinity.

Described as a youth of extraordinary beauty, he has been compared to the Greek hero Achilles, and was recognised as the greatest warrior of the exclusive military brotherhood known as the Red Branch of Ulster.

According to the Ulster Cycle of Tales, it was at a stronghold near present day Armagh that Cúchalainn met and fell in love with the beautiful Emer, described as 'the best maiden in Ireland', because she possessed what were known as the six precious gifts.

These were the gift of beauty, the gift of voice, the gift of sweet speech, the gift of needlework, the gift of wisdom, and the gift of chastity.

Chaste she would remain, however, refusing Cúchulainn's hand in marriage until he had proven himself a mighty warrior.

Accordingly, he set off for the Land of Shadows, better known as the Island of Skye, off the west coast of nearby Scotland, to receive training in the martial arts under the expert tutelage of the famed sorceress and warrior princess Scathach.

His intense training lasted for a year and a day, by which time he had become an adept in several marvellous skills.

These included the apple feat, the thunder feat, the feats of the javelin and the rope, the body feat, the feat of the sword-edge and the sloped-shield, the pole throw, the noble chariot fighter's crouch, the feat of the cat, the leap over the poison stake, the breath feat, the spurt of speed, the stunning shot, and the stroke of precision.

Scathach also presented Cúchulainn with the Gae Bolg, or 'belly spear', a ferocious weapon that, once it was driven inside the victim's body, released thirty deadly barbs that ripped the stomach apart, and a magical sword, known as Caladin.

By the time he returned to Ireland, Cúchulainn had been transformed into a virtual killing machine.

When the battle frenzy took hold of him, it was said that he turned around in his skin so that his feet and knees were to the rear and his calves and buttocks to the front.

To complete this ferocious transformation, it was said that 'one eye receded into his head, the other stood out huge and red on his cheek; a man's head could go into his mouth; his hair bristled like hawthorn, with a drop of blood on each single hair; and from the ridge of his crown there arose a thick column of dark blood like the mast of a great ship.'

A truly frightening sight indeed, and one tale relates the rather odd measures that had to be taken to calm the mighty warrior down when he was gripped by bloodlust.

Threatening the fortress of Emain Macha with his fury, 150 naked women, carrying vats of cold water, were sent to subdue him.

The first vat they plunged him into burst apart, while the second one boiled after he was immersed in it.

The third one, however, only became very hot and by this means Cúchulainn was subdued and the fortress saved.

Another Collins' link to the magical realm of Ireland's Celtic past can be found through the sept known as Ó Cuilleáin – and it is perhaps by no more than weird historical coincidence that the Ó Coileáins relocated to the Ó Cuilleáin territory in present day West Cork in the early years of the thirteenth century.

One theory is that the Ó Cuilleáins derived their name from 'cuileann', a Gaelic word meaning 'holly'.

Considered to embody a special mystic symbolism, and revered by the Druids, the holly tree itself is considered by some to have been symbolic of the genealogy of the descendants of the earliest inhabitants of Ireland.

It is possible that these mysterious Ó Cuilleáins could have been members of the Druidic caste.

As such, they would have preformed several important functions – ranging from acting as teachers and judges to presiding over religious ceremonies involving the 'Old Gods' who were eventually replaced by the one God of Christianity.

The relocation southwards by the Ó Coileáins from North Desmond to the territory of the Ó Cuilleáins in present day West Cork had certainly not been voluntary.

They were literally driven there in the aftermath of the Cambro-Norman invasion of 1169, an event that had truly devastating consequences for native Irish clans such as the Collins.

The Cambro-Norman barons and their retainers had captured Dublin and other strategically important territories by 1171; in October of that year the English monarch Henry II landed on the island at the head of a vast army, intent on curbing the power of his 'Cambro', or Welsh, barons.

Warfare between the two sides was averted when the barons agreed to submit to the royal will, promising Henry homage and allegiance in return for holding the lands they had conquered in his name.

English dominion over the island was ratified in 1175 through the Treaty of Windsor.

Among those Welsh barons who had embarked on the invasion was Gilbert de Clare, Earl of Pembroke, also known as Strongbow.

Among his entourage had been Maurice Fitzgerald, who was rewarded with the grant of lands in Munster, the province that included the ancient territory of the Ó Coileáins in North Desmond

Faced with the overwhelming military might of the Fitzgeralds, or Geraldines as they became known, the Collins sept that had lived there from time immemorial was driven gradually southwards into present day West Cork.

A policy of 'plantation' of loyal Protestants in Ireland began during the reign from 1491 to 1547 of England's Henry VIII, whose religious Reformation effectively outlawed the practice of the Roman Catholic faith in his domains.

This practice of settling Protestants in Ireland combined with attempts to stamp the Crown's authority on the island continued under the reign of Henry's bastard daughter Elizabeth.

This culminated in an attempt to curb the power of feudal lords such as the Fitzgeralds by appointing Crown commissioners to their territories and effectively de-militarising them.

Many of the descendants of the original Norman invaders had by this time become 'more Irish than the Irish', and this was to make for strange bedfellows as they and native Irish families such as the Ó Coileáins frequently combined in revolt to throw off the yoke of the oppressor.

Chapter three:
In freedom's cause

It was not only in defence of their ancient rights and privileges that bearers of the surname of Collins fought, but also for their religion and their nation's freedom and independence.

Born in Cork in 1533, Friar Dominic Collins was destined to become a martyr for his beliefs.

In common with many native Irish who suffered under the harsh penal laws directed against them by the English Crown, he travelled abroad to enter the military service of nations at war with his hated oppressors.

Many became voluntary exiles in France while others, such as Friar Collins, entered the service of Spain.

Serving in the Spanish army for a number of years he later became a lay brother in the Society of Jesus, better known as the Jesuits.

He returned to his native land in 1602, towards the end of the momentous event for Ireland known as the Nine Years War in which a number of mainly Gaelic chieftains and their kin had rebelled against the increasingly oppressive policies of Queen Elizabeth of England.

One of the main leaders of the long and bloody rebellion had been Donal Cam O'Sullivan Beare, who had received financial and military aid from Spain's King Philip II –

Elizabeth's hated Catholic rival and foe.

Philip despatched aid to O'Sullivan in the form of a Spanish invasion force under the command of Don Juan del Águila that landed at Kinsala – and it is possible that Father Collins had arrived with this force.

By January 1602, however, de Águila had surrendered to Elizabeth's Lord Deputy in Ireland, Lord Mountjoy.

Undeterred, the bold O'Sullivan resolved to continue the fight from his native territory in the southwest of Ireland.

It was here that he had the heavily fortified Dunboy Castle, in present day Co. Cork's Beara Peninsula – but it was being held by a force of Spanish troops who were preparing to hand it over, under the terms of de Águila's surrender, to Mountjoy's forces.

O'Sullivan managed to overwhelm the small Spanish force before the handover and garrisoned the castle with more than 140 of his most battle-hardened men, stocking its cellars with arms and ammunition that had been received from Spain.

Having to attend to other pressing military matters, O'Sullivan was forced to leave Dunboy Castle – leaving the garrison under the trusted and capable charge of a Captain Richard MacGeoghegan and Friar Dominic Collins.

A 5000-strong force under the command of the Lord President of Munster, Sir George Carew, was rapidly despatched to take the castle on the heels of O'Sullivan's departure, aided by a naval force that could bombard the fortress from the sea.

The siege of Dunboy Castle began on June 5 with an ear-splitting artillery bombardment from both land and sea that reduced it to near rubble by the tenth day of the siege, and Captain MacGeoghegan was left with no option but seek surrender terms.

The haughty Carew's answer, however, was to hang the messenger who had brought the surrender in front of what remained of the castle walls.

The ferocious artillery bombardment resumed and some of the few remaining defenders desperately tried to reach safety by swimming across to nearby Dursey Island.

Most were captured and killed as they did so, while on the island itself the O'Sullivans who lived there, including women and children, were thrown to their deaths from the cliffs.

Others were burned alive in the island's small church.

Some of the defenders chose to make a last stand in the ruins of Dunboy Castle, including Captain MacGeoghegan and Friar Collins.

MacGeoghegan was killed as he made a desperate attempt to blow up the huge stock of powder in the castle cellars – an attempt that, had it been successful, would have blown not only the attackers into oblivion but also the remaining defenders.

Friar Collins was captured and later hanged in the town of Youghal after being subjected to horrific torture in a vain attempt to extract information.

The rebellion was quashed, but others were destined to

follow, including one that erupted in 1641 over the policy of plantation.

In the insurrection that exploded in 1641, at least 2,000 Protestant settlers were massacred at the hands of Catholic landowners and their native Irish peasantry, while thousands more were stripped of their belongings and driven from their lands to seek refuge where they could.

Terrible as the atrocities were against the Protestant settlers, subsequent accounts became greatly exaggerated, serving to fuel a burning desire on the part of Protestants for revenge against the rebels.

Tragically for Ireland, this revenge became directed not only against the rebels, but native Irish Catholics such as those of the name of Collins in general.

The English Civil War intervened to prevent immediate action against the rebels, but following the execution of Charles I in 1649 and the consolidation of the power of England's fanatically Protestant Oliver Cromwell, the time was ripe for revenge.

The Lord Protector, as he was named, descended on Ireland at the head of a 20,000-strong army that landed at Ringford, near Dublin, in August of 1649.

He had three main aims: to quash all forms of rebellion, to 'remove' all Catholic landowners who had taken part in the rebellion, and to convert the native Irish to the Protestant faith.

An early warning of the terrors that were in store for the native Catholic Irish came when the northeastern town of

Drogheda was stormed and taken in September and between 2,000 and 4,000 of its inhabitants killed, including priests who were summarily put to the sword.

Cromwell soon held Ireland in a grip of iron, allowing him to implement what amounted to a vicious policy of ethnic cleansing.

His troopers were given free rein to hunt down and kill priests, while all Catholic estates were confiscated.

Further rebellions periodically exploded – notably the Rising of 1798 which, again, proved abortive.

But the spirit of rebellion stayed alive and one of the most famous bearers of the name of Collins to have fought for the cause of his nation's independence was Micheál Seán Ó Coileáin, better known as Michael Collins.

Also known as Mick Collins, or The Big Fella, he was born in Sam's Cross, near Clonakilty, in the Ó Coileáin homeland of Cork, in 1880.

A passionate nationalist from an early age, Collins nevertheless moved for a time to London where, in 1906, he sat and passed the entrance examination for that bastion of the British establishment, the Civil Service.

Returning to his native land he became immersed in the growing republican movement and eventually became leader of the Irish Republican Brotherhood.

Arrested after the abortive Easter Rising in Dublin in 1916 he narrowly escaped execution, but spent some time in an internment camp; later, after helping to organise the feared 'flying columns' of the Irish Republican Army during what became the Irish War of Independence, the British government put a massive bounty of £10,000 on his head.

In addition to his military activities Collins also had a number of political roles – including as one of the delegates to the negotiations for the Anglo-Irish Treaty of 1921 that allowed limited self-rule for Ireland.

The Irish Free State was founded in 1922, but faction fighting broke out among republicans over the future course of the new state.

In the bitter civil war that followed, Collins was ambushed and killed while travelling through his native Cork in August of 1922 – and the identity of the assassin who fired the fatal shot has never been satisfactorily determined and even today remains a subject of fierce debate.

His body was brought back to Dublin, where it lay in state for three days.

The colourful life and times of Michael Collins, one of the most famous bearers of the name, became the subject of a movie in 1996 – simply titled Michael Collins – with Irish actor Liam Neeson in the title role.

While some bearers of the name of Collins – such as Friar Dominic Collins and Michael Collins – gained fame through the roles they played at pivotal points in Ireland's history, others have achieved fame in a variety of rather more peaceful pursuits.

Chapter four:

On the world stage

Born Mary Cathleen Collins in Long Beach, California, in 1956 of an exotic pot-pourri of Irish, Welsh, Dutch, and German descent, Bo Derek is the actress who took her surname from her first husband John Derek, the late actor and director who died in 1998.

Her first screen performance was in the 1977 *Orca: the Killer Whale*, while she is also famed for her performance in the 1979 movie *10* that also starred the late Dudley Moore.

An outstanding contemporary actress is **Pauline Collins**, born in Exmouth, Devon, in 1940 and who starred in London in 1988 in the play *Shirley Valentine*.

Her role in the one-woman play transferred to great acclaim to Broadway in 1989, while a film version was released in the same year.

Her various stage and screen performances in *Shirley Valentine* won her a host of awards – including an Academy Award nomination for Best Actress, a BAFTA Award for Best Actress, a Laurence Olivier Award for Best Actress, a Tony Award for Best Actress in a Play, and a Theatre World Award for Outstanding Broadway Debut.

She is also noted for her role as Sarah in the highly acclaimed British television drama production from the 1970s, *Upstairs, Downstairs*, in which her husband John Alderton also starred.

Also on the stage, **Ray Collins**, born in Sacramento, California, in 1889 and who died in 1965, was the actor best known for his role as Lieutenant Tragg in the *Perry Mason* television series that ran throughout the 1950s and 1960s, while **Stephen Collins**, born in Des Moines, Iowa, in 1947 is the American star of stage and screen and also a successful novelist who is married to the actress Faye Grant.

In the highly technical and creative world of film editing, New Zealand-born film editor **Annie Collins** is best known at the time of writing for her work on the hugely successful *Lord of the Rings* trilogy of films – for which she shared a joint Academy Award in 2004 along with Jamie Selkirk for Best Film Editing for their work on *The Return of the King*.

In Australia, **Bill Collins**, born in Sydney in 1934, is the television film critic and presenter who was awarded an Order of Australia Medal in 1987 for his services to television and film.

On a decidedly glamorous note, **Tai Collins,** born in Roanoke, Virginia, is the former Miss Virginia who graced the cover of Playboy magazine in 1991 and who now pursues a career as an actress and screenwriter.

She was the subject of controversy in the same year that she appeared in Playboy, when she alleged she had been involved in a sexual affair with U.S. Senator Chuck Robb while he had been Governor of Virginia – a charge he strenuously denied.

Still in the world of glamour and scandal, **Jackie Collins**, born in Bayswater, London in 1937 is regarded as one of the world's richest living authors – thanks to a range of lurid novels that include the 1983 *Hollywood Wives*, the 1998 *Power*, and *Lethal Seduction*, from 2000.

At the time of writing she is set to publish *Married Lovers*.

Her sister **Joan Collins**, born in 1933, is also an author of novels that include *Prime Time* and *Infamous* – although she is best known as the veteran actress who played the role of Alexis in the Dynasty television series that ran from 1981 to 1989, and in the film adaptations of her sister Jackie's novels *The Stud* and *The Bitch*.

Collins of a rather different literary fame include the playwright and novelist **Wilkie Collins**, born in London in 1824 and a son of the noted landscape artist **William Collins**.

A prolific author, he is best remembered as a close friend of the literary genius Charles Dickens and as the author of *The Woman in White* and *The Moonstone* – with the latter regarded as one of the first detective novels to be written in English.

Crippled with arthritis, Collins became addicted to morphine in the form of laudanum to such an extent that he later admitted to having no memory of writing some sections of his vast literary output.

From the humble start as a publisher of religious books, **William Collins**, born near Glasgow in 1789, founded the Collins publishing empire that in 1990, nearly 140 years after his death in 1853, became the international publishing company of *HarperCollins*.

Publisher of the renowned Collins Dictionary in 1924, Collins also obtained the lucrative licence to publish the Bible, while also publishing early Agatha Christie novels.

In the highly esoteric realms of the paranormal, **Andrew Collins**, born in 1957, is the British author whose works include investigations into the U.F.O. phenomena and the best-selling *From the Ashes of Angels* and *The Cygnus Mystery*.

Billy Collins, born in 1941, has achieved the high poetic distinction of having served two terms, from 2001 to 2003, as Poet Laureate of the United States.

In the world of art, **Ann Collins**, born in 1916 and who died in 1999, was a noted American artist of thoroughbred racehorses.

The world of music contains a distinguished role call of artistes by the name of Collins, including the pop and rock musician and composer **Phil Collins**, born in Chiswick, London, in 1951.

A member of the former progressive rock band Genesis, he now pursues a highly successful solo career that has seen him win a host of musical awards that include an Academy Award for Best Soundtrack for the 1999 *Tarzan* movie.

Born in Cincinnati, Ohio, in 1951, **Bootsy Collins** is a pioneering singer, songwriter, and bass guitarist in the funk genre, while his brother **Catfish Collins** is an innovative rhythm guitarist.

Also in the world of contemporary music, **Edwyn Collins**, born in Edinburgh in 1959, is the founder of the former Scottish band Orange Juice and now a solo artiste.

With a haunting voice that can send shivers up and down the spine, **Judy Collins**, born in Seattle in 1939, is the American folk singer and songwriter who is renowned not only for her musical talent but also for her social activism.

She received a coveted Grammy Award in 1968 for Best Folk performance for her *Both Sides Now*, and another Grammy for her 1975 *Send in the Clowns*.

Moving to the world of hard rock, **Allen Collins**, born in Jacksonville, Florida, in 1952 was one of the founder members of the American band Lynryd Skynrd.

Co-writer of the acclaimed rock opus *Freebird*, he survived a plane crash in 1977 in which other members of the band were killed, and later pursued a successful musical career until his death in 1990.

Known as The Ice Man, and Master of the Telecaster, **Albert Collins**, born in Leona, Texas, in 1932 and who died in 1993, was a celebrated blues guitarist and singer.

On the field of battle, **John Collins** was a recipient of the Victoria Cross, the highest award for gallantry for British and Commonwealth troops, during the First World War.

Collins born in 1881, and who died in 1950 had been an acting Corporal in the 25th Battalion, the Royal Welsh Fusiliers, while serving in Palestine.

He won his V.C. after rescuing wounded comrades from the field and later leading a daring assault on enemy defences.

During the Second World War, **Joseph 'Lightning Joe' Collins** was a renowned American army general. Born in New Orleans in 1896, he died in 1987.

He was the uncle of the American astronaut **Michael Collins**, born in 1930, and who gained fame as the pilot of the command module during the 1969 Apollo 11 moon landing.

His daughter, **Kate Collins**, is a successful actress.

In the highly competitive world of sport, **Doug Collins**, born in Christopher, Illinois, in 1957, is a former American basketball player and announcer who has also coached a number of NBA teams, while on the rugby pitch **Jerry Collins**, born in Samoa in 1980, is the New Zealand player who, at the time of writing, has been capped no less than 38 times for his country.

In European football, **John Collins**, born in Galashiels,

in the Scottish Borders, in 1968, is the former internationalist for his country who is now involved in the management side of the game, while Canadian **Paul Collins**, who was born in 1926 and died in 1995, was a long distance runner who represented his country at Olympic level.

Known as the 'Celtic Warrior', **Steve Collins**, born in Dublin in 1964, is a former world super middleweight boxing champion.

Arthur Edward Jeune Collins, better known as **A.E.J. Collins**, still holds the record for achieving the highest-ever recorded score in cricket – of 628 not out over four afternoons.

He achieved the feat as a thirteen-year-old schoolboy during a match in Bristol in the summer of 1889.

In common with many of his generation, he was killed in action during the First World War.

Key dates in Ireland's history from the first settlers to the formation of the Irish Republic:

circa 7000 B.C.	Arrival and settlement of Stone Age people.
circa 3000 B.C.	Arrival of settlers of New Stone Age period.
circa 600 B.C.	First arrival of the Celts.
200 A.D.	Establishment of Hill of Tara, Co. Meath, as seat of the High Kings.
circa 432 A.D.	Christian mission of St. Patrick.
800-920 A.D.	Invasion and subsequent settlement of Vikings.
1002 A.D.	Brian Boru recognised as High King.
1014	Brian Boru killed at battle of Clontarf.
1169-1170	Cambro-Norman invasion of the island.
1171	Henry II claims Ireland for the English Crown.
1366	Statutes of Kilkenny ban marriage between native Irish and English.
1529-1536	England's Henry VIII embarks on religious Reformation.
1536	Earl of Kildare rebels against the Crown.
1541	Henry VIII declared King of Ireland.
1558	Accession to English throne of Elizabeth I.
1565	Battle of Affane.
1569-1573	First Desmond Rebellion.
1579-1583	Second Desmond Rebellion.
1594-1603	Nine Years War.
1606	Plantation' of Scottish and English settlers.

1607	Flight of the Earls.
1632-1636	Annals of the Four Masters compiled.
1641	Rebellion over policy of plantation and other grievances.
1649	Beginning of Cromwellian conquest.
1688	Flight into exile in France of Catholic Stuart monarch James II as Protestant Prince William of Orange invited to take throne of England along with his wife, Mary.
1689	William and Mary enthroned as joint monarchs; siege of Derry.
1690	Jacobite forces of James defeated by William at battle of the Boyne (July) and Dublin taken.
1691	Athlone taken by William; Jacobite defeats follow at Aughrim, Galway, and Limerick; conflict ends with Treaty of Limerick (October) and Irish officers allowed to leave for France.
1695	Penal laws introduced to restrict rights of Catholics; banishment of Catholic clergy.
1704	Laws introduced constricting rights of Catholics in landholding and public office.
1728	Franchise removed from Catholics.
1791	Foundation of United Irishmen republican movement.
1796	French invasion force lands in Bantry Bay.
1798	Defeat of Rising in Wexford and death of United Irishmen leaders Wolfe Tone and Lord Edward Fitzgerald.

1800	Act of Union between England and Ireland.
1803	Dublin Rising under Robert Emmet.
1829	Catholics allowed to sit in Parliament.
1845-1849	The Great Hunger: thousands starve to death as potato crop fails and thousands more emigrate.
1856	Phoenix Society founded.
1858	Irish Republican Brotherhood established.
1873	Foundation of Home Rule League.
1893	Foundation of Gaelic League.
1904	Foundation of Irish Reform Association.
1913	Dublin strikes and lockout.
1916	Easter Rising in Dublin and proclamation of an Irish Republic.
1917	Irish Parliament formed after Sinn Fein election victory.
1919-1921	War between Irish Republican Army and British Army.
1922	Irish Free State founded, while six northern counties remain part of United Kingdom as Northern Ireland, or Ulster; civil war up until 1923 between rival republican groups.
1949	Foundation of Irish Republic after all remaining constitutional links with Britain are severed.